1 PAGE CONTENT MARKETING

PLAN:Crafting a Smart Content Strategy: Your Easy-to-Follow Guide for your brand

By
Edmund M. Passmore

For permission requests, write to the publisher .

This publication is designed to provide accurate and authoritative information in regard to the subject matter covered. It is sold with the understanding that the publisher is not engaged in rendering professional services. If expert assistance is required, the services of a competent professional should be sought.

Disclaimer

This one-page content marketing strategy's information is meant only for general informative purposes. Although every attempt has been made to present accurate and current information, the author disclaims all express and implied representations and warranties on the availability, correctness, appropriateness, completeness, and reliability of the content found here. As a result, you fully bear all risk related to any reliance you may have on this information.

The author disclaims all liability for any loss or damage resulting from using or relying on the information provided in this one-page content marketing strategy, including but not limited to indirect or consequential loss or damage.

The author's endorsement or suggestion is not implied by hyperlinks or references to third-party websites, goods, or services. The author disclaims all liability for those sites and resources, including any loss or harm resulting from your use of them, as well as any control over their availability, nature, or content.

Every attempt is made to maintain the seamless operation of the one-page content marketing approach. However, if technical difficulties outside of our control cause the one-page content marketing plan to become momentarily unavailable, the author disclaims all liability and will not be held accountable.

It is advisable to seek the opinion of a certified specialist for situation-specific guidance.

Edmund M. Passmore
2023

ABOUT THE AUTHOR: Edmund M. Passmore

Passionate about the intersection of creativity and strategy, Edmund M. Passmore brings a wealth of experience in the dynamic realm of digital marketing. With a knack for transforming ideas into compelling content, they have successfully navigated the ever-evolving landscape of online engagement. .. An experienced narrativeist and marketing aficionado, Edmund M. Passmore is dedicated to helping businesses thrive in the digital sphere through strategic content that resonates with audiences. Stay tuned for more insights and inspiration from this creative mind shaping the future of content marketing.

Conclusion

INTRODUCTION

It's simply a matter of joining the conversation that's already going on in the minds of your target market.

They must be interviewed, ideally via Zoom so that the exchange may be recorded and transcription can be made.

Learn about what's going on in their lives/industry.

Determine what keeps them awake at night.

Then, in your messaging, use their exact words from the transcript.

When the recipient receives your message, he or she should say, "Hey, that's for me."
record the call and transcribe it.

Learn about the events occurring in their lives and industries.

See what it is that keeps them up at night. .

Then use their exact words from the transcript in your message

Chapter one

Determine your target market

A target market: what is it?

A target market is a subset of consumers with comparable needs and characteristics that make them more likely to buy products or services from a business. A corporation must identify its target consumer base before launching its products or services. A business can identify its target market using a variety of methods, such as data tracking, interviewing, and profiling.

Knowing its target market and what motivates them to buy its products or services will help a business succeed more. While it would be great if every client had a universal interest in the things that a firm sold, it is more realistic for companies to determine the precise target market to which their services could be of interest before focusing their marketing, sales, and product development efforts on this information.

For example, a high-end bath products company may decide to target consumers between the ages of 25 and 45 initially. To further define its target market, the company may also wish to concentrate on consumers in that category who appreciate premium and organic products, as this could help the business find customers who are more willing to pay a greater cost for upscale goods. With this knowledge, the business can start creating branding and advertising strategies that convey these values to its target market through the media platforms that this demographic regularly consumes.

How to determine your intended audience

The following six processes will help you determine your target market:

1. Define your proposal.

Determining your offer, or what it is that makes your goods or services appealing, is the first step towards determining your target market. This data makes it easier for you to identify the kinds of customers who could be interested in your offerings. Here are some questions to think about in order to characterize your offer:

• What is your main proposal? You can better comprehend the value your company can offer to your ideal market by defining your primary offer, or your organization's overarching mission with its products and services. Being fully informed about your offer enables you to start considering who could be interested in it.
..
•What issue does it address? When you ask yourself what problem your product answers, you start to realize its worth. An offer gains appeal from customers when it offers a resolution to an issue.

•What makes it superior than the rivals? You may know what your product offers and what problem it answers, but if you can honestly explain why it is superior to what the competition is offering, you'll have a value proposition that will be simpler to sell.

2. Monitor data

Monitoring data-driven analytics is the most straightforward method of determining your target market. Take into account these four methods of gathering data that might assist you in determining your target market:

• Analytics for websites
You may discover who is visiting your website, how long they stay there, and what kind of purchases they make by using analytics data about your website's users. The first step in running a successful web analytics campaign is to provide content on your website that specifically targets keywords associated with your good or service. Your website appears when your target market searches for these terms. These people are being tracked by your analytics, which are gathering data about them. When you gather enough information, you may identify your target market by learning who accessed your content by searching for your chosen keywords.

• Sales and point analytics
The analytics at the point of sale can change based on your business model. Using point-of-sale analytics, firms that sell goods online can find out who bought their goods or services. The disparities between the individual who was interested in your products and the one who actually made a purchase can be displayed by combining point-of-sale and online statistics.

• Online forums
Monitoring data from social media platforms, both automatically and manually, can help you understand what the public thinks about your company and products. On

well-known social media sites, you may conduct a search for your brand or product name to see what others are saying about you. Monitoring this social data can help you better understand and identify your target market in addition to being an excellent approach to resolve complaints or negative reviews. You can learn more about your customers by viewing their public profiles on social media sites when you locate them there.

Furthermore, a lot of social networking sites have their own integrated analytics tools. These tools allow you to monitor article views and responses, which is very helpful when starting a new marketing campaign. By analyzing this data, you may determine the kinds of customers who are drawn to your marketing messaging.

Three. You may better define your target market by defining your ideal audience, especially if you have facts to support some of your initial assumptions. To assist in defining your intended audience, consider these five questions:

1. Who: In your opinion, will benefit from your products? Who is the target market for your goods?

2•What: Which goods do you think these customers would prefer to purchase at this time? What interests, needs, and hobbies does your audience have?

3 • When: What time will your target market utilize your offering? How often and when do they buy goods similar to yours?

4 • Where do your ideal clients reside? Where are they going to use your product?

5•Why: Why will the people who read your stuff buy it? Why is your product superior to those of your competitors?

3. Describe your ideal customer.

When you reduce the size of your audience to a smaller set of people, you are targeting a market. Your target market may be more narrowly defined into a single group or divided into several segments for various items. Consider defining your market by creating a profile of your ideal customer using one of these four market segmentation techniques to learn more specifics about your target audience:

•Create a profile of your ideal client using demographic segmentation, taking into account variables like age, gender, marital status, income, and education. Marketing to married males in their 50s with bachelor's degrees and annual incomes of $100,000 is not the same as marketing to single women in their 29s with doctorates and annual incomes over $50,000. These profiles represent distinct demographic markets.

To create a profile of your ideal client based on attributes like personality, interests, attitudes, lifestyle, beliefs, and values, use psychographic segmentation. Consider the lifestyle, interests, personality, and outlook on life of your ideal client.

Psychographic segmentation can also be supported by the values of your brand. For instance, your ideal client probably symbolizes the fun and creativity that your brand identity—which you developed for your business—conjures up for consumers.

4•Motivations

Create a profile of your ideal customer using behavioral segmentation based on things like brand interactions and purchasing patterns. In keeping with the previous demographic example, if your items are more important to the 29-year-old single woman with a doctorate who makes $50,000 annually, she might nevertheless spend more than the 50-year-old married man with a bachelor's degree who makes $100,000 at your company. To gain a better understanding of the types of people who connect with your ideal client, take a look at the brands of your competitors.

5: Location

To create a profile of your ideal client based on variables like country, region, city, and neighborhood, use geographic segmentation. While some companies operate locally in a single city, others are worldwide. The ability to use regional segmentation to tailor your marketing efforts makes it more likely that the clients and customers who matter most will see your offer.
that the clients and customers who matter most

Content marketing strategy

What is content marketing?

The process of creating and disseminating pertinent, helpful content to draw in and keep your target audience interested is known as content marketing. It frequently denotes proficiency in a certain field and aids in raising brand awareness. Customers desire a brand that they can relate to and that reflects who they are. Relationships may be built and maintained by investing time and energy into creating content that benefits both current and new clients.

Blog articles, videos, podcasts, infographics, emails, newsletters, magazines, webinars, social media postings, template quizzes, and more can all be used in content marketing.

Here are a few notable instances of helpful content:

•Canva's Design School, a selection of quick courses to assist users in making the most of Canva

• Zendesk's blog, which offers instructions and suggestions on sales, customer service, and culture

• Dell Technologies' Trailblazers podcast, which is presented by Walter Isaacson, a history professor at Tulane University and an advising partner at a financial services company, presents unexpected tales of digital upheaval.

•The John Deere The Furrow journal has been published continuously since its founding in 1895. Its objective, which is still to convey entertaining stories and provide practical knowledge, is still the same as one of the first instances of content marketing. When the journal peaked in 1912, it had more than four million readers. The Furrow shows how powerful content marketing can be for long-term consumer involvement and company reputation when it is both entertaining and helpful.

HOW TO CREATE A CONTENT MARKETING PLAN.

Steps To Develop a Content Marketing Plan

You may compare content marketing to searching for hidden treasure. The likelihood is that you will miss the mark if you don't have a map with you.

Thus, in order to actually accomplish your objectives, you must lay up a successful content marketing strategy. Developing compelling content, getting it in front of the proper audiences, and tracking its performance will all be facilitated by a well-thought-out plan.

Are you set to begin developing your plan? For that, too, you'll need a map, which is where this little guide comes in. To get started, just adhere to the top nine stages for developing a content marketing plan.

1. State your objectives

Writing out your marketing objectives is the first step in creating a content marketing strategy.
You have to be very clear about the goals of the marketing plan. It is advisable to document the anticipated outcomes and the implementation schedule.
This will serve as your roadmap for the marketing campaign's launch.

2. Conduct an audit

It's advisable to evaluate prior marketing strategies while building a solid content marketing plan. You must evaluate the past actions of your brand and their level of success.

You can prevent making the same mistakes twice by incorporating what has been effective via this exercise.

3• Create a draft of your plan.

Creating a marketing strategy is the aim of creating a content marketing plan.

Your marketing plan should outline all of the specific actions that you and your group will do during the campaign.

Guidelines for the type of content to be released and the voice in which it should be delivered should also be included.

4• Define roles

No one's job is anybody's job. In order to execute a marketing strategy that works, you must give each member of your team a distinct function.

The precise responsibilities assigned to each member of your team must be documented. It lets you monitor how the campaign is being implemented and identify who is responsible for what

What Does a Content Marketing Plan Contain?

What to look for in a content marketing plan should include the following:

A• Mission declaration

The marketing campaign's objectives are spelled out in detail in the mission statement. It includes a schedule for campaign completion along with the extent of the campaign's operations.

B. Marketing data

Customer satisfaction data have to be included in a content marketing plan.

Data on the demographics of the target audience should also be included. This would assist you in determining the needs of your audience and helping you to better grasp what they desire.

You might also provide information about the marketing activities of your rivals.

The campaign's established key performance indicators (KPIs) should also be made explicit in addition to this. The measurements you should use to assess the success of your media campaign are these KPIs.

C•Strategy market plan

Without a content marketing strategy, a plan for content marketing would be lacking. The campaign's recommended course of action is outlined in depth in the content marketing plan.

There are specifics on the kind of content that will be utilized, the schedule for the campaign, and the roles that each team member will play.

Your marketing team will use this as a guide during the campaign.

Content Marketing Planners' Role

The person in charge of creating a brand's content marketing plan is known as the content marketing planner. A content marketing planner's responsibilities include:

Content accountability

The content included in the marketing campaign is the planner's responsibility. The campaign's success or failure is mostly determined by the content that is used.

They must ensure that the material speaks to the target audience's pain points and aligns with the brand's ethos.

Project and team management

The execution of a brand's content marketing strategy determines its success. The project needs to be managed well for this to occur.

The team and the marketing project are under the content marketing planner's direction.

They must be capable of encouraging teamwork and possess excellent leadership qualities.

In order to make sure the marketing campaign stays within its allocated time and scope, a content marketing planner must also keep a careful eye on the project.

To assess the success of the content marketing strategy, they must also routinely check the KPIs.

How to Develop a Strategy for Content Marketing

time online with the aid of an effective content marketing plan.

Thus, investing the effort to create a winning strategy for your brand is very worthwhile. Here's how to finish it.

1. Be well-aware of your target market

For your content to have the biggest impact, it must relate to your clients' needs, desires, and dreams. You must be intimately familiar with your target audience in order to achieve that.

Buyer personas and tasks to be completed are two methods for understanding your target audience.

Using buyer personas, you may paint a portrait of your target market by outlining their:

•Characteristics
•Favorites and enmities
•purchasing patterns
•Important issues
•Reasons for
•By concentrating on the cause behind the customer's decision to engage with your brand, Jobs to be done provides further insights into their behavior.

2. Analyze competitors and benchmarking

You must first ascertain where you and your rivals stand right now before you can forward with developing a plan.

You can make decisions that are better than ever with that information.

Examine your content performance first. Evaluate how well your current content is reaching your target audience and consider how you may improve. Do you have any industry keyword rankings? Could you get a better rank?

After that, focus on the content marketing initiatives of your top three rivals.

Ask each one of them:

To what extent does their content cover each topic in detail?
For which keywords do they regularly score highly?
Does their material encourage social media shares?
Simply use all of that information to help you create your content marketing strategy.

3. Look up industry terms

It's definitely time to finish up whatever keyword research you haven't already done for your brand.

As lighthouses, keywords point potential buyers in your direction for each pertinent search.

To help with that journey, your content needs to contain relevant keywords in all the proper places.

Every piece of content should actually have a primary keyword of its own as well as supporting semantic keywords.

Even though it might seem intimidating, you can easily finish your keyword research with the help of online tools like SpyFu, SEMrush, or Google Keyword Planner.

Alternatively, you could just get right to the point and get a content strategist to do the legwork for you

4. Establish the plan's KPIs and objectives.

Your opinion is not a reliable indicator of your content's overall success, regardless of how you personally relate to it.

Instead, you must use objective measurements, sometimes referred to as key performance indicators, to gauge its effectiveness.

In the field of content marketing, the most widely used ones are as follows:

•Views of Engagement Pages
•Duration on page
•Sessions' pages, comments, and conversions
•generating of leads
•Rates of conversion
•The acquisition cost

•Income from investment
•Credibility
•Linkbacks
•Shares on social media
•Influencers' mentions
•ranking of keywords
You get to decide which metrics to track. Just be careful to select a few from every level. Next, make goals, achieve them with great success, set new objectives, and repeat.

5. Decide which content kinds are best for you.

There's no one-size-fits-all method when it comes to content creation. Each brand must determine which kinds of content will most appeal to its intended audience.

To effectively target the market during the awareness, contemplation, and decision phases of the buyer's journey, you must also modify the material you offer.

Content types to take into account at each stage include:

•Being Aware
•Sites
•Visual Aids
•movies
•posts on social media
•Pages that land

•Considering
•Email correspondence
•Electronic Books
•Online seminars
•Live footage
•Synopses
•Selection
•Case Reports
•Ideas
•Highlights of features
extended articles
•The price pages
•Remember to provide lessons, blog pieces, and FAQ pages to ensure that your consumers get the most out of their purchases.

6. Choose the appropriate channels for distribution

Wherever your customers spend their online time, that's where your content needs to be. If not, it will simply disappear into the digital void, unnoticed and unheeded for ever.

Customers will find your material through search thanks to your keywords. However, that is not all you need to do. Makee a plan to proudly market your content across all the media that your target audience prefers.

You'll need to know which social networking sites they prefer in order to do that. Additionally, ascertain whether they will interact with guest articles, SMS contact, or email newsletters.

Next, write your content, post it on your website, and aggressively market it.

Don't be afraid to advertise each piece again and again. After all, you never know when your readers will have the opportunity to click through and interact with your content.

7. Create an excellent content schedule.

This is where you assemble the whole puzzle: your content calendar. Making the right content creation and distribution easier, that move plots out your route to success.

Start with a monthly schedule for content so you can determine what is most effective for your brand. If you'd like, you can next proceed to making quarterly calendars.

Title and objective
Type of content
primary term Internal connections
Date of publication Channels of distribution
After that, all you need to do to complete your plans is mark the dates of the content release on a calendar.

CHAPTER 2
: LEAD NURTURING

SBA statistics indicates that almost one-third of companies with employees fail in the first two years of operation. This article will discuss one of the key components of business success—consistent lead generation—but it won't go into detail about the many reasons a firm could fail.

You need to become proficient at obtaining business leads if you want your organization to grow profitably and scale swiftly.

In marketing, what is lead generation?
In marketing, generating actionable consumer interest in your company's products is known as lead generation. This usually entails a client striking up a discussion or giving you their contact details so you can follow up on the goods or services your company offers.

For instance, in order to provide business leads, a law company could get:

•A potential customer submitting a form to inquire about their services.

•A prospective customer calling to schedule a consultation.

•A direct social media message inquiring about their prices.

•A request for a consultation by email from a prospective customer.

Therefore, creating a marketing experience that makes it simple for clients to interact with your organization is a part of generating new business leads. If you've heard of demand generation and are asking if you actually need lead generation or demand generation, the answer is that you need both and it's not worth separating the two at this time.

Your lead generation tactics should always lead to a face-to-face meeting or the exchange of a prospect's contact or payment details.

Twelve Lead Generation Instances

Having a business lead generating strategy in place will help you convert strangers into paying clients, regardless of whether you intend to purchase leads or develop your own lead generation marketing plan.

Use these 26 lead generation strategies to boost sales and expand your company right now. Get your free eBook right now!

Look into the next 12 ways to generate leads for your business before developing a plan.

1. Direct Communication

In marketing, what is lead generation?
Direct communication is a fantastic way to bring in new customers if your company offers high-end goods or services that are paid for on a monthly retainer. It is preferable to rule this

choice out if low-value, high-volume sales are the foundation of your income model.

If it appears that a prospect would be a good fit for your company, you can get in touch with them personally via phone, email, social media, or even in person.

For instance, if you own a Houston-based lawn care business and a huge commercial building is being constructed nearby, get in touch with the property manager to discuss maintaining the finished estate. This is an excellent illustration of lead generation in Houston, or any other place that your local company might serve.

2. Utilize LinkedIn to Create Leads

It may surprise you to learn that the buying power of the LinkedIn audience is twice that of the typical web audience. LinkedIn is a very useful tool for B2B marketing, and it may produce incredibly lucrative outcomes.

Developing business possibilities can be facilitated by establishing connections with influential leaders in the sector. A potential client could become your next paying client if they approach you for recommendations regarding a service you provide.

If you have the funds, using social media for advertising is another excellent approach to take advantage of LinkedIn. Even better, you can choose to pay for lead gen advertisements that feature forms right there in the advertisement. Relevant users can easily sign up for your products or services with the help of these advertising.

Making connections with people in your target demographic on LinkedIn, commenting on their posts, and sending them a direct message to pitch your goods or services is another strategy to obtain business leads. Be aware that this strategy will only be effective if their posts and profile suggest that your offerings will assist them address one of their unmet needs. If that isn't the case, people may disregard your outreach as spam, which would damage your reputation.

3. Use retargeting and advertising techniques for lead creation Texas

There are other places besides social media to market! To promote to search engine users, use Google or Bing's tailored pay-per-click advertising. This facilitates the serving of advertising for queries that you already know are highly pertinent to your company.

Consider yourself a BMW dealer in Houston attempting to enhance your automotive dealership's marketing. Ads targeting terms like "new BMW in Houston" or "best BMW dealer in Houston" can be made, and you can even use a geo-filter to target users who are searching in the Houston region.

On their initial visit to your website, very few visitors convert. You can use display retargeting to show visual adverts for your items on other well-known websites throughout the internet when a user clicks on one of your PPC ads.

While it may take some time to get right, digital advertising has the potential to be one of your company's best sources of leads.

4. Request Referrals from Present Clients

One of the earliest lead generation marketing techniques available is customer referrals. Encourage a satisfied consumer to tell their friends about your product or service so that others may also benefit from it.

Customers may perform this task for free if your company's offerings are of sufficient quality, or you may implement an incentive program. Give your clients a particular percentage off their subsequent monthly retainer price, for instance, for each new client they recommend.

Because they are profitable and your present customers are doing the majority of the effort, client referrals are a terrific strategy to grow your business's lead generation.

5. Compose Guest Posts

One of the best ways to increase your SEO and get referral business through content marketing is to write guest articles.

Guest posting provides the following marketing benefits:

establishes new industry ties
increases your SEO by obtaining high-quality, backlinks from industry-relevant sources.
produces traffic through referrals from a pertinent audience
By writing guest posts for websites that are related to your sector but don't directly compete with you, you can generate leads for your company. If you run a marketing company, for instance, you may write guest blogs for nearby sign companies. You are aware that the people who buy signs want to market themselves, and your services are a nice addition to that.

Guest writing for local influencers is consistent with local SEO best practices. Your website will rank higher in that locality if, for instance, a well-known podcaster in your area writes a guest blog and gives you backlinks.

Make sure the website you're guest writing for is pertinent to your location and industry for the best results.

6. Get a high search engine ranking to produce leads

ways to produce leads for your company
Make sure your target audience can find you with ease when they search for your goods or services online.

Learn how to use SEO and SEM for your website to generate more leads for your business.
To find out what terms your target audience searches for before acquiring your good or service, start by conducting keyword research.

To locate search data, you can utilize programs like Google AdWords Keyword Planner or SEMrush.

Optimize the content of your page after you've chosen the appropriate keywords. It could be challenging to rank organically if you're selling a good or service that faces intense competition. If you're ready to invest, using an SEO provider can be a terrific approach to produce consistent leads.

Before you make any financial decisions, find out how to select an SEO business. Since not all agencies produce the same outcomes, it's critical to understand how to pick the best one for your company.

7.Responding to forum enquiry

One excellent technique to demonstrate your subject matter expertise and establish reciprocity is by responding to forum inquiries. This technique can assist you in finding leads in a matter of minutes if used strategically.

This passage from Influence at Work describes how being the first to give something can help you receive something of equal or higher value.

Apply this persuasive theory by responding to forum queries on websites such as Reddit or Quora. Choose a category that pertains to your company, then begin responding to inquiries from users. Don't forget to include a call to action at the conclusion of your response encouraging the user to utilize your product or service to assist solve their problem.

Consider, for instance, that you run a legal practice that specializes in family law. You can join a legal subreddit where people post queries that are especially related to the services that your company provides. Every day, set aside a short period of time to look for any questions you can answer with some knowledge.

If someone asks a question regarding child support, provide a helpful response, link to your website, and recommend that they get in touch with you for a consultation. By providing free legal advice, you could encourage the person who posed the issue to pay you for future legal services.

In addition to being a terrific way to create new company leads, responding to forum inquiries can also help with SEO. In instance, for our Reddit example, your link may benefit your law firm's SEO if your child support response receives a sufficient number of upvotes. Your lead generation activities may yield compounding rewards with this kind of synergy.

8. Provide a Free Resource or Lead Magnet

One of the best ways to create business-to-business sales leads is by providing a free tool. What kind of issue is resolved by your product or service? Is it possible to provide a helpful product at no cost to users that does not require them to make a purchase from your company in the end?

For this instance, let's say you are a plastic surgeon practicing in Houston. Users are curious to know about procedure prices and recuperation timeframes, you find after conducting a Twitter audience poll and conducting some keyword research.

Consequently, you make the decision to put up an eBook that lists all of the various operations you offer along with their pricing ranges, recovery times, and before and after photo examples. After creating a blog post teaser, you ask readers to provide you with their name, phone number, and email address in exchange for the information you've supplied.

Your blog post can start collecting contact information if it has the appropriate topic, targeting, and call to action. A greater conversion rate is the outcome of the blog topic, CTA, and offer being more aligned. Based on blog lead conversion data from Databox, these are the average visit-to-lead conversion rates that you should anticipate.

Blog conversion is the most effective technique for businesses to get leads.
Because of how beneficial the teaser blog article is, curious readers are linking to your website and registering for the free eBook. Your advice will benefit your Houston plastic surgery SEO while also assisting you in generating leads for your company.

What opportunities are there in your sector? Creating calculators, gathering original research, providing free guidelines, or even providing free consultations are a few common examples of how to generate leads for your company.
Aws
acquire more leads for your company in Houston Speaking with influential people in your field can help you and your company grow significantly. This is not only a fantastic method to learn from professionals in your field and

expand your network, but you can also utilize these interviews to produce impactful content.

You can choose to podcast your interview, create a Q&A blog post, or video record it. By structuring your interview in these many ways, you can make the most of the information and attract visitors to your website or social media accounts. To increase the amount of business leads you get, you might even think about gating the interviews and asking for contact information.

The influencers will frequently distribute the final interview through their marketing platforms, expanding your audience and return on investment.

9.Networking

While it rarely generates income directly, networking is excellent for fostering career chances. Make an effort to choose a networking event that is relevant to your industry and located locally. This will guarantee that you are taking advantage of simple business victories and assist you keep your trip expenses down.

What are the potential benefits of networking? You will nearly always be let down if your only concern is the return on investment. Rather, search for indirect victories.

Perhaps you'll run onto a complementary company that you can collaborate with to exchange leads and broaden your reach. Maybe you approach an influencer who agrees to do an interview with you, allowing you to create a fantastic piece of content and reach a wider audience with your marketing efforts. Even opportunities for your business to guest blog can arise from networking.

One of the finest ways to obtain leads for your business is by networking, as there are virtually always numerous returns on your investment.

10. Make an Offer via Email

It's not always necessary for lead generation to result from reaching a new audience. Your email lists may contain unrealized business opportunity.

If you have an email list of your own, you might want to create a special offer. A one-time deal or exclusive discount can successfully convert a passerby into your next paying client.

Additionally, you can send exclusive email offers to email lists owned by other persons. By actively networking or forming partnerships with firms that compliment yours in your field, you can arrange a deal that will allow you to advertise to their clientele.

Remember our earlier example of a marketing firm and sign manufacturer collaborating on a guest blog? The marketing firm might pay the sign maker 5% of all sales made as a result of the campaign and recommend a business promotion in the sign company's upcoming email blast. For the marketing company, the sign company, and the contented new consumers, this is a win-win scenario.

11.Follow blog of competitors

I should tell you that I did not keep the best lead generating technique for businesses for last.

As a company owner or marketing executive, you should make it a point to follow blogs of competitors as well as trade journals. This can provide you opportunity to be helpful and help you stay on top of your competitors' movements.

Provide your own thoughts in response if you see that people have left multiple unanswered blog comments on a certain topic. Including a call to action that directs readers to pertinent content on your website that can further address their questions is a good idea.

When attempting to obtain business leads via blog comments, proceed with caution. Because blogs are vulnerable to spam, it can be challenging to post comments that are sincere. Furthermore, you might offend your rivals by headhunting their audience.

To find out what terms your target audience searches for before acquiring your good or service, start by conducting keyword research. To locate search data, you can utilize programs like Google AdWords Keyword Planner or SEMrush.

Optimize the content of your page after you've chosen the appropriate keywords. It could be challenging to rank organically if you're selling a good or service that faces intense competition. If you're ready to invest, using an SEO provider can be a terrific approach to produce consistent leads.

Before you make any financial decisions, find out how to select an SEO business. Since not all agencies produce the same outcomes, it's critical to understand how to pick the best one for your company.

When attempting to obtain business leads via blog comments, proceed with caution. Because blogs are vulnerable to spam, it can be challenging to post comments that are sincere. Furthermore, you might offend your rivals by headhunting their audience.

OBTAINING LEADS

Need to provide a consistent flow of leads for your sales team to stay busy? Here are five methods to ensure the success of your lead generating.

1. Prepare your go-to-market plan.

The go-to-market (GTM) strategy for your business includes valuable details on how to prioritize your lead generation efforts and determine the kind of leads you require. For example, it can indicate which markets to target and provide details about your ideal customer profile (ICP), or the target market that will most benefit from your good or service.

Before you proceed with lead generation, you should have a GTM plan in place since, without one, you'll be shooting in the dark. You won't be aware of which areas to concentrate on, which leads are worth pursuing, etc. Thus, begin by developing a GTM plan if your team does not currently have one.

2.analysis

Now that you have a GTM plan as a backup, it's time to get your hands dirty, which entails doing research. One of the most crucial aspects of your lead generation efforts is research.

Your GTM strategy serves as a road map, outlining the people you must contact and providing instructions on how to do so. However, you now have to work out the details, such as:

How can I discover my ICP? You must ascertain the locations and types of material that your target clients frequent in order to respond to this. Which occasions do they often attend? Which accounts do they follow, and what podcasts do they listen to? Although Sparktoro is a helpful tool for audience research, you'll still need to look into other options. Examine your rivals, learn about market trends, and participate in internet forums.

How can I better earn the time of my ICP? Do you need to nurture them with tailored material, or should you just send them an email giving a free demo? These strategies may be effective, depending on the buyer's level of awareness. When attempting to qualify leads, you must present yourself in the best possible light and make use of all available channels. And sound research informs these choices.

3. Apply a tool for prospecting

You can identify your ICP by using the extensive datasets available in prospecting tools. You can narrow down your search by using various criteria, including those based on company size, area, industry, and more. Leads can be further filtered based on seniority, tenure, job titles, and other criteria.

Formally speaking, there are three methods for sorting and filtering leads:

•**Make use of demography**. This information relates to the attributes, such as age and gender, of a specific population group.

•**Firmographics are used.** This comprises information that can be used to categorize an organization, such as the size, location, industry, and other specifics of a business.

•**Technographics are used. This** information relates to the technologies that an organization utilizes, how widely it is adopted, and how much it costs. If you sell technology or tech-related services, this data is extremely useful. If you're selling Salesforce development, for instance, you can locate businesses that are currently utilizing the platform or something comparable. Additionally, you may utilize a site like BuiltWith to locate businesses that use Shopify or WooCommerce if you offer tech to e-commerce stores.

4. Begin contacting and qualifying leads.

Now that you have all the necessary research, marketing materials, and contact details, it's time to start contacting leads and gauging their interest. There are several methods for achieving this, and your strategy will change based on whether you want to produce:

• Outbound referrals. These are leads that you approach directly; for example, leads that you find via social media direct messages, cold calls, or cold emails.
arriving leads. Your inbound marketing strategy, or your lead-generating marketing campaigns, is what brings these leads to your company. Those that attended one of your recent virtual events, for example, may be inbound leads.

Let's concentrate on outgoing leads for the time being; we'll talk about how to create inbound leads in the following section. To obtain outbound leads, follow these steps:

• Begin by making prospects. Recall the topics we covered in the preceding section. Locate possible leads and get their contact details. Speak with them. Direct mail, cold phoning, cold emailing, and social media are your primary possibilities. You may improve your chances of producing leads by using a variety of channels.

• Eligible leads are forwarded to the sales team after qualification. Which leads are interested in your offer and have responded well to your outreach? When it comes time to seal the deal, engage them even more and generate revenues. For assistance with your outreach, you can also look at these lead generating resources.

5. Begin utilizing inbound marketing.

As sales is busy generating outbound leads and expanding your business through all those new deals, now is the right moment to start the arduous but worthwhile process of creating inbound prospects. And there're numerous methods to go about this. The majority of companies combine short- and long-term tactics.

•**Campaigns for performance marketing** are typically the fastest approach to produce leads. Pay-per-click advertisements on social media sites can be used to target inbound leads through personalized content and experiences. You may gather information from leads or compel them to act by using these tailored advertisements.

•**Performance marketing initiatives** can help you swiftly create return on investment, but they're not as simple to implement as they initially appear. You will have to:

•**Resolve expenses**. You are investing money to generate revenue when you run advertisements, so you must be careful not to waste it. For instance, your ad spend isn't producing a quantifiable return if it's producing low-quality leads that don't become paying clients. If, on the other hand, you're paying a lot of money (in comparison to industry benchmarks) to get new leads, you may need to reconsider your campaign and assess its effectiveness. Ensure the details are correct. This calls for appropriate copy, offer, and creative. You'll need eye-catching images for the creative that draw in your viewers. Your copy's messaging must be relatable to your target audience, address their issues, and inspire them to act. However, a poor proposition cannot be sold by even the best copywriters or creatives. Prior to anything else, you must develop an offer that captivates and truly benefits your target audience.

•**Continue testing.** Seldom do businesses get everything right the first time; the greatest outcomes are usually obtained by ongoing testing of various ad variations, results measurement, and campaign optimization. To properly implement performance marketing, you'll need a team that is mature because these are some hefty requests.

To produce leads, you can also spend in various long-term plays in addition to performance marketing. Although these plays won't yield results right away, they will eventually assist you in producing a steady flow of leads that are of a high caliber.

The following are a few of the best long-term inbound marketing strategies:

• **Purchasing SEO.** Directly generate leads from search engines (mostly Google, however Bing is also helpful for particular companies and sectors).

• **Spending money on advertising.** This could involve setting up a billboard, running advertisements on social media, running Google Ads, or utilizing a variety of advertising platforms.

• **Organizing webinars or events**. To establish your credibility and pique people's interest in your goods or services, share insightful information with those in your sector.

• **Direct mail or email advertising**. gold but ancient.

• **Producing or contributing to a podcast**. Having your own podcast is a terrific method to position your business as an authority in the field. If your team isn't prepared to tackle a project of this magnitude, you may alternatively consider scheduling key executives for well-known podcasts in your sector. They may spread the news and tell your tale.

As you can see, there are many various approaches of generating inbound leads, therefore it's critical to choose which ones are best for your company. Through study and trial and error, you'll discover which tactics and channels work best for your company.

Once you've established what works, scale back to create an unending lead flow.

6. Put in place a referral scheme

Customers are more inclined to refer others to your business when they truly enjoy your product or service. And one of the best ways to swiftly create new leads is to ask for referrals. Asking your devoted clients to recommend you is all you need to do at times. However, if your goal is to use referrals as a reliable source of leads, you should consider putting in place a structured program.

• **By offering rewards for referrals**, you can encourage your most devoted clients and strongest supporters to assist you in gaining new business. For successful recommendations, you may, for instance, pay them a cut of the profits from the new clients they bring in or a discount on your goods or services.

•**Higher-quality leads** can also be produced with the aid of referral marketing. As per the

State of Referral Marketing research by SaaSquatch, recommended customers:

• Show 18% greater fidelity to your company
Increase your spending on goods and services by 13.2%.
possess lifetime values 16% greater than those of non-referred clients.
These figures will vary according to the industry you work in. However, referred clients usually meet these remarkable numbers.

•Another intriguing element that supports the success of your referral program is time, as revealed by Ambassador's B2B Referral Marketing by the Numbers report. According to their analysis, B2B businesses who made long-term investments in referral programs saw growing returns over time:

Thus, recommendations not only aid in the rapid generation of leads but also have the potential to increase revenue over time!

Are you prepared to produce leads for your company?

It takes effort to set up a system that will continuously produce leads for your company, but as they say, Rome wasn't built in a day (or even a week). Therefore, even though it will take some time to do your homework, get your hands dirty, and learn from mistakes, the benefits are worthwhile.

CHAPTER 3:

POSITION YOUR BRAND

What is brand positioning?

A brand's positioning describes the distinct value that it offers to its target audience. It's a tactic used by brands to communicate their value proposition—the reason a buyer would choose their company over competitors—while establishing their brand identity. Furthermore, brand positioning is employed when a business wishes to present itself to its target market in a particular light so that consumers would associate the brand with its value proposition.

A brand positioning statement:
what is it?

An internal positioning summary known as a brand positioning statement is what businesses use to explain and highlight the benefits that their brand offers to both target markets and consumers. It is employed as a means of clearly stating the value proposition of a brand. Brand positioning statements should strike a balance between aspiration and reality since they are typically a component of a bigger marketing plan.

The following factors need to be taken into account when developing a brand positioning statement:

• Who is the intended clientele or market?
•In which category do you offer goods or services?
•What is your product or service's biggest advantage and impact?
•What is the evidence for that impact and benefit?
Companies can differentiate themselves from competitors and, more crucially, offer their brand's

value to customers by providing a clear value proposition in their brand positioning statement that addresses these issues.

What makes brand positioning crucial?

For a business to effectively communicate to consumers the value that their brand offers, brand positioning is crucial. This occurs through a brand positioning statement used internally as well as through a variety of marketing methods used externally and linked to by the brand positioning statement. To be realistically relevant, brands should talk about their value proposition and target consumer in their brand positioning statement.

Advertisers may tie their display advertising strategy with their brand positioning by sharing their distinctive brand insights with Amazon's Sponsored Display audiences.

How is a brand positioning strategy made? Depending on the size, mission, and market niche of the brand, there are several approaches that businesses can take to developing and implementing a brand positioning plan.

• Recognize the present placement of your brand.
•Identify the special value that you offer.
• Determine the positioning of your rivals.
• Draft your statement of positioning.
• Assess and verify that your placement is effective.
• Strengthen what makes your brand unique.

The aforementioned steps are meant to assist brands in identifying the specific benefits that customers will receive from their product or service while also delving deeply into what makes their brand special. By concentrating on the benefits that companies can provide to their intended audience, they may develop a compelling brand positioning plan that appeals to consumers.

Samples of how brands are positioned

Let's examine a few well-known companies that have successfully used brand positioning to reach their target demographic as part of a bigger brand strategy.

• McDonald's positioning as a brand
McDonald's distinguishes itself from the competition by offering its patrons consistently

high-quality meal items and first-rate service throughout all of its locations. The way the brand portrays itself speaks volumes about the company's commitment to enhancing its operations and to pleasing its clients through subliminal customer satisfaction.

•Dove's positioning as a brand
Dove distinguishes itself through its personal care products by emphasizing women's true, natural attractiveness. Through the usage of their products, all women can embrace their real selves, according to their brand positioning approach. Dove positions itself in a way that resonates with their customers and makes an effect through brand campaigns and other marketing strategies.

• The brand positioning of Disha Publications
Disha Publication, a major force in the publishing industry, has established its reputation as a reliable name across a variety of academic subjects on Amazon by running sponsored advertisements. Disha Publication's sales soared thanks to sponsored advertisements, which also helped to improve their brand positioning on Amazon.

Recognize your rivals

Understanding your industry's rivals and the goods they sell will help your company stand out. Any serious business seeks to know who their competition are. With this knowledge, your firm will be able to better position its product pricing in the market and develop more effective marketing strategies.

Your business performance will soar as a result of the marketing strategies you might develop based on your understanding of your competitors' shortcomings in the marketplace. Determining the risks that both new and established competitors offer to your company's development is also essential.

In the business world, you must be aware of your rivals and understand how to use this information to your advantage.

What information about the rivals do I need to know?
Lucrative companies are always monitoring how their rivals operate. The following details are what

you should be extremely interested in learning about your rivals:

The CEO, the owner of the company, and their personality; Products and services and how they are sold; Product pricing; Distribution and Delivery; Customer Loyalty Systems; Innovations in Business Methods and Products; Employee Count and Skill Levels; Utilization of New Technologies; Annual Reports (Public Companies); Media and Marketing Activities.

You must learn as much as you can about both your rivals' clients and competitors:

Who are their customers, what goods do they buy from the marketplace, and what qualities and flaws do they perceive in them?
either long-term or short-term clients.
Further investigation into their clientele's data may reveal details like:

Who are the target customers of your competitors?
If rival companies create new, superior items;
Competitors' financial resources and capital.
How can I make use of the competitor information?

First, it is necessary to assess the data that has been collected on them. This procedure will inform you of any gaps in the market that your rivals haven't managed to close. You can take advantage of those precise spots.

Conversely, your market research report will show you whether certain market categories are overly saturated, indicating that you should shift your attention elsewhere.

Compile a list of all the details you have discovered about your rivals. Next, arrange the data into categories. What can you gain by studying your rivals? Are you able to outperform them? Do they have any areas where they fall short of your performance?

Who are your competitors

Understanding your industry's rivals and the goods they sell will help your company stand out. Any serious business seeks to know who their competition are. With this knowledge, your firm will be able to better position its product pricing in the market and develop more effective marketing strategies.

Your business performance will soar as a result of the marketing strategies you might develop based on your understanding of your competitors' shortcomings in the marketplace. Determining the risks that both new and established competitors offer to your company's development is also essential.

 In the business world, you must be aware of your rivals and understand how to use this information to your advantage.

Who competes with me?

Nowadays, a firm cannot exist without competition. For instance, if you run a steakhouse in a small town and your customers prefer to spend money at pubs, movie theaters, and other associated businesses, you will still have to compete with them.

However, as more people are using the Internet to buy goods and services, you aren't just up against regional companies anymore. Businesses from other cities and nations are also competitors of yours.

They might sell goods that are comparable to yours, which would hurt sales of yours. However, competition is more than just stealing from you. In the event that some of your new rivals wish to sell their businesses to you or want to sell their products with your assistance, you could also benefit greatly financially and in terms of market share.

For this reason, you must continuously conduct market research to identify potential rivals.

What information about the rivals do I need to know?

Lucrative companies are always monitoring how their rivals operate. The following details are what you should be extremely interested in learning about your rivals:

Products and services and the means by which they are marketed; Product pricing; Product delivery and distribution; Customer loyalty programs; Innovations in business practices and goods; number of workers and level of experience; use of new technologies; the CEO's and the business owner's personalities;

reports for the year (public firms);
marketing and media initiatives.
You must learn as much as you can about both your
rivals' clients and competitors:

Who are their customers, what goods do they buy
from the marketplace, and what qualities and flaws
do they perceive in them?
either long-term or short-term clients.
Further investigation into their clientele's data may
reveal details like:

Who are the target customers of your competitors?
If rival companies create new, superior items;
Competitors' financial resources and capital.
How can I make use of the competitor information?
First, it is necessary to assess the data that has been
collected on them. This procedure will inform you
of any gaps in the market that your rivals haven't
managed to close. You can take advantage of those
precise spots.

Conversely, your market research report will show
you whether certain market categories are overly
saturated, indicating that you should shift your
attention elsewhere.

Compile a list of all the details you have discovered about your rivals. Next, arrange the data into categories. What can you gain by studying your rivals? Are you able to outperform them? Do they have any areas where they fall short of your performance?

CHAPTER 4:

WHO ARE YOUR CUSTOMERS

Customers are well understood by successful organizations. Identifying your target market is the

first step in creating a campaign that works.
Additionally, you may offer your solution at the
appropriate cost, at the appropriate location, and in
their native tongue when you comprehend the
unique traits and requirements of your clientele.

You can quickly outperform your competitors if you
gain more knowledge about your clientele.
Going gently today will help you move rapidly later.
You can determine and unleash your clients'
potential by providing the answers to the following
questions.

Which kind of client are you looking for?
The kind of clientele your firm seeks is mostly
determined by the nature of the enterprise and the
sector it serves. For instance, a company selling
expensive goods must undoubtedly target clients
with higher income levels. A mass-market retail
establishment, however, caters to a distinct clientele.
Analyze the features of typical consumers of
products similar to those your firm sells and the
industry you operate in before deciding on the kind
of customer you want for your business.

While doing so, take into account the following qualities:

Their characteristics:

• Age, gender, ethnicity, income bracket, and location

After you've identified the kind of clients you want to work with, evaluate their various purchasing patterns to identify which will probably be most beneficial to your company.

• Frequent buyers; semi-frequent buyers; one-time buyers

Do certain clients provide your company with greater value than others? In 1906, Vilfredo Pareto devised the "80/20" rule. According to the rule, 80% of your revenue should come from the top 20% of your clientele. You should probably concentrate on this group of customers.

•How much money do you hope they will bring in?

You can put your company strategy through its paces by projecting revenue from your ideal client. After all, marketing typically costs money in addition to time. It is not a free endeavor.

Are you aware of how much money each client pulls in for your company? This simplifies the process of determining the appropriate expenditure for gaining those customers.

Consider the expenditures associated with obtaining each client in addition to overhead when calculating your return on investment. It can indicate that you are overspending or that you have good reason to raise your marketing budget.

•Recognizing the importance of your product to your customers and their lives
Knowing exactly who your clients are and how your product fits their demands will make marketing easier. While knowing the general customer's demographics is important, it also makes sense to conduct qualitative and quantitative research on their attributes. You can do this in several ways:

•Know Your Current Clientele - Consider the clients and customers that mean the most to you. Are there any traits in common?

•Use surveys and questionnaires to get feedback from customers about how they use your product or what features they find most valuable.

• Examine the Comments or Frequently Asked Questions section. Do you see any common problems that people want you to solve?

• Make Use of Social Media: Social media's interactive features allow you to interact with users and develop a profile of your clientele.

•It's also critical to comprehend how your product affects their lives. And over time, this can alter. You could divide up your clientele according to this:

• The casual consumer: These purchasers utilize a product from time to time, but they don't use it frequently or give it much thought.

•Motivated customer: These are customers who are really driven to use your product and who value it greatly in their lives. Because of this, people frequently conduct in-depth research on a product before making a purchase.

•Customer with a lifestyle focus: These individuals link your product to the kind of lifestyle they currently lead or hope to lead. For these kinds of customers, the image of the business and the product are crucial.

How can you contact them each day?
- What channels do they make use of?

To contact your customers, you must be aware of their attributes and characteristics.

The ways that different generational groups consume media vary. For instance:

♠Baby boomers: For news and information, this group typically turns to printed materials like newspapers and magazines as well as traditional media like radio and television. Although some people utilize social media, they usually don't use it as their main source of media, unlike many millennials. Because of this, a campaign aimed at this demographic might not be as heavily focused on social media as one aimed at a younger demographic. In addition to less interactive online marketing strategies like email marketing, which can reach this demographic for less money than traditional media, conventional media marketing sources should also be taken into account.

♦Millennials: As a generation, they are far more likely to rely on social media, in one form or another, as their primary media consumption platform. A portion of this population has even "cut the cord," solely consuming media that is delivered online and given up on traditional media. A marketing plan focused mostly on social media and utilizing little to no traditional media can effectively target this demographic.

♠Generation X: This generation is situated between the baby boomer and millennial generations in terms of age and media consumption patterns. They maintain a foothold in both camps, so your efforts

that incorporate components from social media and conventional media can succeed with them.
How can you get them to become clients?
There are several ways for your consumers to contact you. Cost-effective strategies for converting strangers into consumers are included in organic acquisition. It could happen through word-of-mouth, outreach on social media, or inbound marketing strategies like a compelling blog post that draws readers in and puts you in a good position for when they're ready to buy.

Techniques for organic acquisition are a crucial component of your marketing. Through social media, search engines, and your blogs, the individuals you are targeting find you. This indicates that they are "qualified," and your efforts in creating messages and content contribute to the development of credibility and trust. On the other hand, even if these methods are "unpaid," they can take a long time to produce results.

The strategy you use for campaigns will depend on your marketing objectives.

Think about the following elements:

•**Campaign timeline**: Paying for leads might be the best course of action if your campaign is intended to produce results quickly. Organic techniques like social media outreach, email list development, and content marketing can yield substantial rewards over time, but they usually take months or even years to show a noticeable effect. Therefore, the most efficient strategy for achieving quick results is probably to use paid marketing initiatives like search engine marketing (SEM), buy email mailing lists, or use classic advertising methods like TV, print, or radio ads either by themselves or in conjunction with organic efforts.

•**Campaign budget**: Organic outreach initiatives are a terrific option and should be the mainstay of your marketing activity if you have a small marketing budget. By doing this, you may continue to pursue organic efforts while making judicious use of paid marketing efforts where they are most needed.

• **Relevant audience**: You will reach a larger portion of your consumer base through organic techniques if they are currently using social media for communication. Positive experiences with products or businesses are more likely to be shared online, especially by millennials, and word-of-mouth gains momentum when it is appreciated and shared. To get the word out about your items, choose the channels that will work best for your audience.

Understanding and knowing your clients is essential for running a successful business and can provide you with a competitive edge. You can better serve them with your product or service, market to them more effectively, and improve their purchasing experience. You'll have a better chance of drawing in new business if you take the time to get to know your loyal customers.

THINGS THEY WANT

Discover the top 10 elements that affect consumers today, regardless of whether they are making an online purchase, looking for a service-based solution, or making in-person purchases.

• **Mastery.** Customers of today desire discretion over what they purchase and how they are advertised to. This indicates that consumers desire options, and not only for products.

•**a range.** Additionally, they want choices on how to interact with you through various marketing platforms. If you don't give them an option, they will automatically choose something that doesn't benefit you.

•**Value:** Value encompasses more than simply cost. It has to do with what buyers believe they receive for their money. Customers of today are dubious.

They won't trust a product if the price looks too low. They will believe they are being taken advantage of if it is excessively high. It is up to you to locate that sweet spot.

• **PERSONAL RECOMMENDATIONS**: In the modern world, a consumer can ask hundreds of individuals a question regarding a product and receive a dozen recommendations in a matter of minutes. Here loyalty is important. You'll have the best marketing money can buy when you give your customers a cause to refer you.

• **One-of-a-kind encounters:** Chain stores are becoming obsolete. Personalized is in. You can offer distinctive experiences either directly through your product offering or indirectly through the way you portray it. "What can you do for me?" is a question posed by your clients. They should not have to settle for a prefabricated response.

•**Service:** The unseen product is what you provide. In an industry where all other criteria might be deemed equal, service stands out as the one area where your business can differentiate itself. Excellent service is not something that just happens. It needs to be fostered, emphasized, and taught daily. Productivity. Customers of today desire more than simply quick service. They want things completed correctly and promptly. Increasing employee productivity is a top-down procedure. It begins with policies established by the business, passes via management, then reaches staff members and, at last, clients.

•**social accountability**. Customers are requesting to collaborate with businesses that align with their values more and more. Over 50% of consumers today are willing to pay extra for things they believe to be socially conscious. This is a growing number of consumers.

•**Association**. Discovering the points where your story and theirs overlap can help you build relationships with your clients. Instead of the other way around, make them the protagonist of your tale.

Using stories to connect with clients converts them into devoted fans. Information. Your customers anticipate an answer if they have any questions. This includes inquiries about basic product knowledge, ongoing services, and—possibly most importantly—solutions to their issues. In order to provide clients with the information they anticipate, you must proactively provide your team with the necessary knowledge.

fidelity. You are already aware that retaining loyal customers is essential to the success of your company. You should also keep in mind that your clients look to you for loyalty. Hold yourself to your promise. Avoid giving too much away and not enough. Be truthful.

Delivering what your customers need starts with knowing what they want. It won't be simple. Developing a loyal customer base must be a component of your continuous training program for staff members and, more significantly, your company culture.

CONCLUSION

To sum up, this one-page content marketing plan offers a concise road map for navigating the ever-changing world of digital content. Your brand can create a meaningful online presence by defining clear goals, comprehending the target market, and carefully producing and distributing content through appropriate platforms. Consistently evaluating data, gathering input, and adjusting to changing patterns will guarantee a dynamic and successful content strategy that connects with your target market and enhances the overall performance of your advertising campaigns.

REVIEW

To Whom It May Concern,

I hope this communication finds you in good health. I would want to take this opportunity to thank you for taking the time to study the one-page content marketing plan. I am so grateful for your support.

Would you consider taking a moment to write a review if you were pleased with the book and think the information was valuable? Not just to me but also to other readers who might be thinking about getting a copy, your comments are very valuable.

You can post a review on any platform of your choice, including [Online Retailer] and [Goodreads]. Your candid opinions will raise awareness of the book and assist readers in realizing its potential.

Again, I want to thank you for joining me on this trip. I value the time and thought you have given me.

Sincere greetings

Edmund M. Passmore